Acknowledgements

My dream to empower people and elevate them [...] best and noble lives would have been a long time [...] the love, support and the selflessness of my incre[...] Terry Napora. My potency is as strong as it is bec[...] you believed in me and elevated me. Thank you ... I will love you forever!

To my daughters Kharrissa, Amber, Larissa and Shannon – you inspire me daily, to be my best self. You enrich my life with your courage, fortitude and strength and I am so honoured to be your mom. Thank you for sharing me with the world ... I will carry you with me always!

To my family and friends who have walked with me through many fires and helped me choose my responses – I am so grateful.

Brooke Leyenhorst - what a gem you have been. You came into view at the right time to support me with this layout and make this project a reality. I am so grateful for your help.

"Truth is always good currency and has no expiry date.
It works no matter when it is used."

-Abby Napora

Vitamin A Dose Instructions

Vitamin A is known for its role in supporting healthy bone development, it is critical for the optimum functioning of the immune system, and keeps the skin and mucus cells healthy. It is an effective antioxidant as it neutralizes free radicals in the body that cause cell and tissue damage. It is useful in combatting viruses and is a critical contributor to good vision.

I see my role in people's lives to be much like the multipurpose, multidimensional and multi-focused work of Vitamin A. I am committed to your mental, emotional and overall physical health. Challenging thoughts that are distorted and unhealthy are much like the oxidative value of Vitamin A. It encourages you to live to your potential and serves to keep your trajectory towards optimum mental and emotional health. This assists you in building your immunity and equipping you with skills and tools that work to keep you healthy and engaged in life in meaningful ways, as well as developing and sustaining a healthy perspective while maintaining a clear vision for your life.

I encourage you to begin your journey with me with these goals in mind. As you read your daily dose, pay close attention to how your thinking is being challenged, what in the dosage is making you uncomfortable and what adjustments you need to make in your thinking and behaviour that will move you closer to the life you envision for yourself.

Think of this as a three month project. Read your daily doses morning and evening and write your reflections at night just before you go to bed. Be committed to this regimen for 31 days. After you have completed the first round, start the regimen over, but this time notice how your reflections and thoughts have changed. Finally, in your third round of taking your daily dose of Vitamin A, tune into how your perspective and behaviour has changed and then celebrate these changes as rewards to your commitment to your personal growth and development.

Day 1

Your eyes determine the path your vehicle will follow. New drivers are trained to keep their eyes on the road as a way to ensure safety and develop their skills. This cultivates a discipline that help new drivers manage distractions. Similarly, in life, if you want to get to your goals and achieve the quality of life you want to have, then you have to learn to manage distractions that are bound to derail you. Hope goes into your future and issues you an invitation to join it there. If you want a hopeful, fulfilling and joyous life, you must choose to stop allowing your life circumstances to put you in autopilot. This mode leaves you focused on what's not working, how you failed, who rejected you and how you can never achieve your goals. Consider this an alarm signal going off in the cockpit of your life, alerting you to the danger of self-sabotage, isolation, depression and anxiety. Get back to the instrumentation panel of your thought life. Reset your coordinates towards happiness, hope, empowerment and freedom and then keep thinking these thoughts over and over again until you arrive at your new destination. Once there, repeat this process to stay out of the danger zone.

Reflection

Am I in autopilot mode responding to life by rote and doing what I have always done?

Yes I was until last weekend @ the ladies retreat where I felt something open up + shift in me to make room for trusting God + others.

What am I focusing on?

Focusing on finding a safe "box" where I can protect myself from pain + try to control my own life. ie. Not being vulnerable, not participating in church / bible study, expending so much energy to try and find a job I am familiar with.

How can I change what I am looking at to move towards the life I want to have?

Instead of looking ahead and seeing the negative I need to see possibilities in the unknown. I need to begin to trust God + other people again and walk with the assurance that with God all things are possible.

"Be present" – stop thinking of and living in the future. "If it feels good, do it." "Just enjoy life. You have a right to be happy." These words are the social rumblings that flow down the streets we live on, through the doors of our lives, influencing our psyche, and guiding how we choose to live. On their own, these words are attractive and liberating, but in context these words carry a certain recklessness and carelessness. Previous generations bear the legacy of working hard, being future focused, and fearing lack. They did not live present and available lives to their families. Today, we have to ask ourselves how far has the pendulum swung, and how far off balance are we? When we enter our future selves, are we going to find provision for our personal health, our relationships, our sexuality and our finances? Or will we enter a season of bankruptcy where we are searching for value and meaning because we only lived in the moment?

Sow to where you are going. Invest daily through your everyday choices toward your future self. Deposit in yourself today the self-respect, integrity and value you wish to have tomorrow. Don't take your health, your sexuality, and your abilities for granted. Make conscious current investments that will bear dividends for your future self because it is known that we cannot draw out of someone else's account without getting into trouble. Live responsibly today with your tomorrow in mind because "Out of sight is out of mind."

Reflection

What is my current responsibility to my future self?

To invest in my emotional + spiritual health so that I can be a positive role model for my children. I want to learn to walk through difficulties clinging to God + finding joy + praising Him. My future is in His hands I am done trying to control it.

Do I live in the present while responsibly preparing for my future regarding my finances and my mental, emotional and physical health?

Day 3

Courageous living is becoming a rarity. We live in a world where we are conditioned to reach for quick fixes, take shortcuts and avoid pain at all costs. We fight from behind computer screens and other social media avenues, more comfortable with our voices being heard than our faces being seen. Although anonymity seems appealing, one cannot live this way without personal impact. Thinking systems are activated and patterns become entrenched in us when we live lives that lack courage. ***Lacking courage to address things outside of ourselves is only an indicator that we lack courage to address things within ourselves.*** We are critical of our world and others because we are first critical of ourselves. We express hate and disdain for others because of our own self-hate. It takes courage to face these dark places within ourselves instead of cowardly projecting our "darkness" on others. You can cultivate courage. Work on challenging your fear and discomfort thresholds. Take a risk. Do what you have always longed to do. First, work on loving yourself. Take steps to address those things about yourself that you dislike. Go with courage to those "dark" places within yourself so that you can courageously face the challenges outside of yourself. Live courageously today - and tomorrow you will find that you are braver, bolder and more resilient.

Reflection

Do I live courageously? I'm not afraid to take risks + put myself out there except when it comes to writing. There I am not courageous.

What prevents me from living courageously?

Fear of rejection + criticism

What can I change to begin my courageous journey towards the life I desire to have?

Trust in the Lord and not my own judgement. Let Him lead me and clear the road for me to follow.

Teach me the art of trusting in God. Help me to relax and maintain complete confidence in you. Hour by hour and day by day.

Day 4

Many people are experiencing anxiety and burnout because of their belief in the unspoken social code at work. "You must make it on your own," as needing help is considered "weakness." This way of thinking is counter-intuitive and counterproductive. When we are in distress we are wired to turn to those we love for comfort and safety. We, are designed for community. Drawing on your community in time of need helps you re-anchor yourself and allows your community to live to their purpose of being able to support and strengthen you. It is said that, "Just like Success = Love + Persistence, Failure = Ego + Persistence." Fearing to call out for help when you need it most is not strength, it is weakness. The characteristic that governs this behaviour is pride. ***Pride will resist progress and sabotage your desire for connection.*** Resist that sense to take care of things on your own even when you are beyond exhausted. Make a courageous choice to walk humbly (not weakly) and ask for help today!

Reflection

Do I struggle to ask for help?

Yes because I deeply believe that I am responsible for self preservation from pain / hurt / weakness.

What prevents me from asking for help?

My strong desire for self preservation

Why is it important that I ask for help?

Because if I don't ask then I trust no one. I can't trust others = I can't trust God.

Today my prayer is to ask for God's help to hold me secure when others do not come through for me. Hold me tight Lord, like a parent comforts their child.

Day 5

The things we don't know hurt us and undermine our ability to make necessary changes to become the type of people we want to be, and to create the type of life we want to have. We are familiar with the saying that "Ignorance is bliss". This saying captures the apparent passive and artificial sense of well-being that exists for those who choose to remain ignorant because they stand in the way of their own evolution. Learning comes with the responsibility to assimilate what we learn into our lives so that we move from unconscious and avoidant behaviours to thoughtful and intentional choices in order to change and grow. Those who are "unconsciously incompetent" lack awareness and insight into what is needed for change. Being unaware essentially shows that you are out of tune with yourself and those around you. The things you don't know hurt you and undermine your ability to make necessary changes to become the type of person you want to be. Awareness and taking responsibility become the key ingredients for change that will move you towards bliss. Instead of resisting the light of awareness that wants to break in on you, embrace it. Cooperating with this awareness brings with it a natural energy that steers you towards responsible and blissful living.

Reflection

What have I chosen to be ignorant of in my life?

How much my emotions influence my action.

Has this choice made me happy and enhanced my life?

NO.

What can you do to move from ignorance to blissful living?

Pray about my feelings + become aware of why they are there + how to better manage them.

Continue working on my relationship w God even though I don't "feel" like it.

Day 6

Perspective is that ability to see things in the context of their environment. Prejudicial thinking often leads us to form opinions without bothering with the facts. We judge things through our filter of preference, level of comfort and opinion. When we do this, our perspective is skewed because we judge facts through a filter that alters what we are looking at. The filter, or perspective, by which we view a matter, is superimposed on the "actual" experience so that the reality and facts appear distorted. If you find that the same type of misunderstanding and conflict is re-occurring in various relationships in your life, it is likely that you are looking through a lens which colours the facts. A change in perspective will allow you to see the facts in the context of their reality. Distortions will give way so that you are able to make informed and healthier choices. This way you break old and dysfunctional patterns as you begin to view your world differently.

Reflection

Am I in the habit of forming opinions without bothering with the facts?

Are there recurring themes of relational conflict in my life?

What do I need to change in order to see situations for what they are?

Day 7

Re-framing is a technique used to replace a negative thought with a factual and positive one so that challenges can be viewed differently. It is how *facts are preserved and assumptions are confronted.* Assumptions are the frames that limit your capabilities and your perception of self. When you change the frame, the power of the assumption or false belief is destabilized, and often broken as the structure that holds a belief together is challenged and can no longer support that belief. A thought or a situation that often arises for me is "I cannot reach anything". The frame or belief that holds this statement together is **"being *short limits me*"**. If I re-frame by saying "Dynamite comes in small packages", I am not denying my small/short stature but I have changed how I see my smallness. Just as necessity mothers invention, re-framing mothers possibilities and causes you to see situations through alternate and creative ways. If you are able to re-frame, then you can create new ways of thinking. Instead of seeing the situation as impossible you can say, "This conflict gives us the *opportunity* to find new ways of relating". This re-frame shifts you into a new place and instead of withdrawing from the conflict and feeling hopeless, hope is unlocked and creative solutions and strategies come into view.

Just as necessity inspires innovation and invention, re-framing dismantles supporting beliefs around limiting thoughts and causes you to shift into new perspectives and creative thinking zones.

Reflection

What challenges am I experiencing currently?

What do I believe about the challenges I am facing?

How can I change the frame around what I am looking at?

Day 8

Have you ever noticed that people who focus on the negative things in life are grumpy, hard to be around, and do not like themselves very much? It does not take much for them to revert to their negative and grumpy states, where even a harmless look from a passerby can be interpreted poorly and they find themselves immediately in a state of discouragement. The brain of this person is responsive to that familiar negative thinking and feeling pressure, much like how a memory foam mattress responds to the familiar weight of a person. The great news is that our brains are responsive and malleable and can be trained to respond to different ways of thinking. By training your brain and changing your mind, you are able to defy your genetic predisposition. You don't have to be like your angry mother and depressed father. Research is showing that the longer you stay with a happy memory, the longer you allow your senses to absorb the effects of that happiness, then the easier and quicker it is for you to get to that happy place again. This is true for when people say, "That just took me to my happy place". What is your happy place?

Reflection

Be present and think about the kind of thoughts you think.
Are they negative thoughts?

Are they thoughts of limitations?

Are they possibility thoughts?

What stops me from thinking positively?

Day 9

It does not cease to amaze me how, as human beings, we will do whatever we can to avoid "our struggles". The contradiction here is that we were born through struggle. Every contraction is precipitated by pain. New life is only possible with a commitment to focus and a will to push through the pain while cooperating with the contraction. Any woman who has given birth knows that resisting the contraction can result in compromising the life and health of both the baby and the mother. When we cooperate with the contraction, it makes for safer and healthier outcomes for mom and baby. To cooperate with the contraction means to embrace the pain in a way that allows your body to do what it was created to do - to bring forth new life.

Reflection

Do I resist struggles and challenges in my life?

What is the value of co-operating with the life contractions I am experiencing?

Day 10

Thankfulness is much like co-operation in that they both require that we embrace what we need to embrace when we need to embrace it, so that we can shift from where we are to where we need to be. You will never know what you are capable of if you constantly resist your struggle. Struggle is a life contraction that is designed to bring you into a new place. The more you resist it, the harder life will be. You will not only compromise your strength but the new life you incubate. Embrace the struggle in a way that will allow your body, mind and spirit to enter this new place that is designed to reveal your strength, bring you joy and fulfillment, and allow you to experience new life. That thing that you have been resisting, give it a big embrace, welcome its challenge, co-operate with the pressure of formation that accompanies it and see the new you emerge into a new place. So many opportunities await you there.

Reflection

What is the value of embracing my struggle?

What have I been resisting?

Day 11

Potential is dormant power. The implication is that the capacity to grow and become exists within each person. It is up to the individual to determine whether or not their potential will be realized. An acorn has the potential to become a mighty oak. Within it lies the sleeping power of greatness. The way to its greatness is unlocking, accessing and releasing the power within itself. Why do some acorns remain acorns and why do others become oak trees? The acorn that becomes a tree burrows itself into the earth where the darkness and pressure cracks the shell so that it attracts to it all the nutrients it needs to grow. As its potential germinates beneath the earth it begins to muster the energy to break through the wall of its darkroom incubator to find the sun so that it can continue on in its quest to become that great tree. When the acorn becomes the mighty oak we know that it has lived to its potential. Similarly, you have this power asleep inside of you. It is up to you to find the right environment to burrow yourself into so that this latent power can be awakened. It is up to you to push through barriers and obstacles so that your creativity, dreams, ideas, talents, innovation and service is unlocked, so that every ounce of greatness trapped within you is released.

Reflection

Are you living to your potential?

What prevents you from accessing this dormant power within you?

What can you do today to begin to unlock, access and release this trapped power to move you towards the greater you?

Day 12

More and more people have a longing for meaningful connection. This innate desire for depth and quality of relationship has no discrimination. Those who are single and those who have partners desire genuine relationships that offer safety, validation and confirmation of self-worth and value. Here individuals are free to be themselves and authenticity is celebrated. Guardedness in relationships is how we tend to self-preserve once we have experienced hurt and betrayal. It also becomes a barrier towards establishing deeper and stronger bonds. Choose to challenge what you "feel" with what is "true" about those in your world right now. Don't avoid people who care about you because you fear rejection, particularly when they have consistently shown you that they care. Risk being authentic. Challenge feelings of anxiety by disputing the mind trap that "if people really know who I am then they will not like me". People are attracted and gravitate towards authenticity. Being untrue to yourself by pretending to be someone you are not becomes unsavoury ingredients for deep and abiding relationships. This is an excellent litmus test that will help you discern who meaningful relational contributors in your life are. Observe the relationships in your life. Note those who *confirm* your worth without you having to perform for it. Now observe those where you have to act and be a certain way. How do you feel? What sensations do you experience in your body? Those who ***confirm*** your value and celebrate your authenticity are those who you allow to remain in your life because *"those who come into your life and give you value are those who can take value with them when they leave your life".* True relationships should never leave you depleted.

Reflection

Do I desire deep and meaningful relationships?

How can I cultivate these types of relationships?

What is MY criteria for keeping some relationships closer than others?

Day 13

As long as behaviour is justified, it cannot be corrected. The greatest value in gaining freedom from certain behaviours is acknowledging its existence in your life. Situations and circumstances do not "cause" you to be angry, jealous, lazy, rude, impatient or aggressive. They typically reveal who you are in those circumstances. Failure to acknowledge these traits and their existence in your life will allow them to continue to have influence and control over you. Many people are owned by anger, fear, pride, insecurity, jealousy and inferiority because they refuse to own or acknowledge that these existed in them long before they were triggered and exposed by external circumstances. What triggers you is in you, and is a wonderful clue to what needs to be owned by you so that you can live responsively instead of reactively.

Reflection

Why is it important for me to acknowledge harmful behaviours that are active in my life?

What will happen if I don't "own" these behaviours?

Day 14

In a world where perfection is an ideal that most aspire to, failure is seen as an enemy and something that opposes success and happiness with a whole bunch of shame attached to it. The culture of the day is that failure is to be avoided at all costs. Somehow, over the years, failure has come to be seen as a happening or an event that limits, depletes and devalues a person's worth.

Milton Erickson wrote that, "Life will bring you pain all by itself. Your responsibility is to create joy." This got me thinking about how failure brings with it a responsibility. *The privilege of failing allows for the greatest growth if we choose to learn and grow.* Every negative experience in your life, such as financial stress and relationship failure, all become the vehicle by which learning can occur. If you see failure as a teacher and embrace the lesson within each experience, you will shift to a new place, a different place and bigger place. You will be enlarged and your potential will be unlocked. When failure is seen as an enemy, holding patterns of frustration, anger, and fear emerge, that shrink and diminish the world of those who will not embrace the value housed within the experience of failing.

Reflection

Why is failure a friend?

How has my perspective of failure changed?

Where in my life do I have to embrace failure?

Day 15

Embracing the things and events in your life that has caused you the deepest pain and the highest stress, as noble teachers and fine friends, is the first step to "creating joy". Strength and wisdom become the products of deepest failures when you embrace the lesson within the pain and the failure. Life offers you the richest passage to learn about who you really are in these fragile, yet powerful, moments. Embracing the work of failure will process you in ways that success never will. Failure actually goes to work for you. You may dislike the discomfort that accompanies its presence in your life, yet embracing it as a friend sets you up to ascend, to shift and to become your true self. In this way, failure becomes a clue of what you must get through in order to become who you are meant to be - your best and original self!

Reflection

What is the purpose of failure?

How can I benefit from failure?

Day 16

The quickest and easiest way to manage what currently manages you is to be courageous and brave enough to recognize that what is triggered in you exists in you already. Become curious about your reactions - don't disown them. When I owned that anger that existed in my life, I stopped being owned by it. I was empowered to manage and redirect its expression in useful ways rather than being governed by it. Placing blame on others and circumstances is typically how anger expressed itself through me. I stopped holding up my visa to being angry and began to confront its presence in my life. I was no longer clueless. At the end of the day, "It's not what you swallow that pollutes your life, but what you vomit up". What you own about yourself you can change. In the words of Antoine de Saint-Exupéry, to live this way "Is to be slowly born". Owning the things about ourselves that we dislike or are ashamed of inadvertently causes us to give birth to our new selves. New patterns replace old ones and living a totally new and different life is possible.

Reflection

What am I triggered by?

Where do my reactions originate - inside or outside of myself?

Day 17

Most of us have great capacity to be empathetic, yet we struggle with how to support those we love when we have not experienced loss as they have. The quality of connection between people is not contingent upon shared experiences but on your ability to connect and identify with that raw human essence in the core of each person's struggle, and how they respond to this extension of care and empathy from you. Avoiding people's pain because you have not experienced it interrupts our human design to serve and heal each other through our humanness. While we cannot fix their pain, being present with those who are hurting can give them the will to fight and the courage to endure, and allow us the privilege to grow and heal together.

Reflection

Am I awkward around those who are hurting?

Do I avoid them? Why?

What can I do to connect with others in their pain?

How will this enrich my life?

Day 18

Many are exhausted and worn out because they have not developed the skill to accept the things they cannot change. When you choose, for example, to accept that a relationship has ended, that you made a poor investment, or that a loved one is sick, the *acceptance itself gives you power to no longer be trapped by the powerlessness of your circumstances.* By accepting that a relationship has ended, you are empowered to position yourself to take what you learned and prepare yourself differently because you have clarity about what you actually want and deserve in any future relationships. However, when you do not accept that a relationship has ended, you become a victim to all the things that you wish you had said but never did. In a sense, *your lack of acceptance keeps harming you because you are trapped in an ending that never ends without any room for a new beginning.* The progression is subtle and if you are out of sync with yourself, you may miss the power and progression that comes with acceptance.

Reflection

Do I struggle to accept the things I cannot change? Why?

How has my view of acceptance changed?

Day 19

After acceptance, comes courage and wisdom. Wisdom is the correct application of knowledge. Wisdom will increase your ability to discern how to effectively respond to your challenges. Acceptance, which may appear to be very passive at first glance, is actually a dynamic force that has the power to propel you out of an unpleasant situation into something hopeful, beautiful and transformative. The willful surrender that acceptance requires of us is often misinterpreted as weakness and "giving in". Agitation and despair are often the fruit of this misinterpretation and counters the freedom and joy which are the fruit of true acceptance.

Reflection

Is acceptance a passive choice and action?

Why is acceptance important?

Have I confused acceptance with weakness?

How has my view changed?

Day 20

There are so many social trends these days that living responsively to them can cause the most stable among us to become destabilized and unanchored. Just because it is a trend does not mean that it is right. I encourage you to stop and think about your present responsibility to your future self. Goofing off at school or university is not being responsible to your future self, eating without self-control will have future health consequence, a lack of activity will impact your physical strength and endurance, and living unconscientiously and dis-invested in your mental and emotional health will find you reaching for something that does not exist when you enter your future. Previous generations may have been on the other end of the pendulum, being so future-focused and working so hard that they did not lead present and available lives to their families. The blight of this generation is that we have swung to the other end of the pendulum, living life so fully present that many are showing up in their 30's and 40's relationally, emotionally, and financially bankrupt.

Reflection

What is my current responsibility to my future self?

Have I lived conscientiously to date?

Day 21

Living in a healthy tension is a life principle that allows you to be present and purposeful, as well as visionary, with a vested interest in your future. A kite without a string is a kite that will never fly safely. It will be earthbound until it flies and if it resists the string in flight it will either crash into trees or powerlines to its demise. A kite that understands the value of a string held at the right tension is able to soar and dip and parade its splendour in the skies. Individuals who understand, respect and integrate this principle of a healthy tension into their lives tend to be successful at navigating life without crashing and burning.

No one turns 65 years of age and expects to receive a pension without having paid into a pension fund, or becomes ill and expects employment insurance to pay them an income while they recover, if they have not contributed to EI. For these benefits to be available and accessible, they require that, at one time, individuals seeking compensation have responsibly contributed to these funds. These individuals invested in their future selves.

Many people are experiencing financial bankruptcy, impulsively going after what they wanted and not what they needed. Others are relationally bankrupt, having used up their sexuality as currency, and are at a time in their lives where they desire meaningful relationship and connection but are unable to secure the quality of relationships they wish to have. Living without this principle of a healthy tension throws our lives out of harmony. For balance to return the tension must be embraced and with practice you will learn that you cannot spend more than the money you have, you cannot truly love others without first loving yourself and you cannot be accepted if you are busy judging.

Reflection

What is the value of embracing the principle of a "healthy tension."?

How have I resisted this tension in my life and what has been the consequences?

What steps can I take to be present and purposeful and to be future focused?

Day 22

Do you find yourself saying "yes" all the time to all requests made by those who matter in your world? Are you exhausted physically, mentally, and emotionally? Do you find it difficult to say no? When you say no, do you ruminate and worry about what those you have said no to are thinking of you? Then it is very likely that you believe that your self-worth is regulated by your performance and what others think of you.

When this distorted sense of self is accommodated, you will do whatever you need to, to try and alleviate the pain and discomfort of being devalued. It is difficult to say "no" when saying "yes" will bring you the validation, affirmation, and recognition you need to feed this inaccurate sense of worth. Saying "yes" out of obligation and fear of disapproval, is different than saying "yes" because you want to. Saying "no" because you are self-focused and uninterested in helping is different to saying "no" because you understand your value and have insight into how saying "no" when necessary preserves your worth and personal integrity. What you say "yes" or "no" to become the regulating valves to asserting and affirming your value.

Reflection

Do I perform to gain worth and value?

Why do I do this?

What can I do to begin to change this behaviour?

Day 23

Understanding the value of boundaries is the best gift you can give yourself. When healthy boundaries are set, they preserve that space for you to continue to do your work to become who you want to be, and makes a demand on those around you to respect the requirement you set in place to maintain your health. Most fear setting boundaries because they fear losing relationships or creating distance in their emotional ties with those they love. The opposite is true. Boundaries question and bring clarification to the type and quality of bond you have with those you relate to. If your bond only exists with a friend around talking about and criticising other friends, then that bond needs to be inspected in light of what emotional health and relationships mean to you. If you choose not to do this inspection, it is highly likely that you will ever feel safe in that relationship. Setting boundaries keeps you safe and redirects others to do their own work. Setting boundaries is like putting on a hazmat suit. It allows you to be in toxic environments where you can offer support and assistance without compromising your own health by succumbing to and being overcome by others' inability to cope with their own emotional toxicity.

Reflection

Do I set healthy boundaries in my relationships?

Have I become a dumping ground for others' toxic emotions?

What can I do to change this?

Day 24

If you are feeling overwhelmed and emotionally exhausted it is likely that your boundaries are permeable. You may be a dumping ground for people who cannot manage their own toxic emotions and need to release some to you in order to relieve their own mental and emotional pressure. If you allow yourself to be the noxious release for others then what you are doing is enabling these individuals to make room for more harmful emotions without any personal accountability. Their process to deal with the issues that need attention in their lives is interrupted and stalls because of your enablement. Setting boundaries keeps you safe and redirects others to do their own work.

Reflection

What happens to me and to those who I allow to "dump" their toxic emotions on me?

Day 25

Individuals who constantly draw you into their "drama" or highly toxic emotional conundrums can be likened to mudslinging matches. When you engage in this activity, you are muddied, disoriented, confused, feel attacked, and are exhausted from trying to find solid ground under your feet. You leave this type of interaction feeling hurt and vulnerable, vowing to yourself that you will never succumb to this convoluted way of interacting again. Inevitably, you do because individuals who love drama are highly skilled at drawing you into it. Their specialty is having the right bait with your name attached to it. They will use your low self-esteem, your need to help, your fear of failure or your need for approval to lure you into their toxic traps for the purpose of disarming you and increasing self-doubt in you so that you serve their agenda. There is a way where you can emotionally disconnect from these relationships. It is where you consciously choose to observe behaviour without being sucked into it. Identify their tactics and patterns and refuse to take the bait. Visualize yourself as an observer watching the show and refuse to become an actor in their "reality shows".

Reflection

Do I get sucked into other peoples' drama?

Am I exhausted in some or all of my relationships?

What can I do to observe others' behaviours without being drawn into them?

Day 26

Forgiveness is the ability to discharge yourself from the act and the person who harmed you so that you are free to heal and make different choices for yourself. The distorted thinking that exists for many is that you need the person who harmed you to ask you for forgiveness in order to heal. Though asking for forgiveness is ideal, it is not necessary. Some people wait a lifetime and go to their graves waiting for someone to apologize, having being held hostage to the person and circumstances. When forgiveness is extended, whether asked for or not, you choose to no longer allow the offending person to have power over your days and your life. You stave off the places where you hemorrhage emotional and mental energy and conserve strength for efforts that can improve the quality of your life. When you choose to forgive and release others from the mental and emotional debt that they owe to you, you get to access benefits such as physical health and overall well-being as a result of this choice.

Reflection

Am I mentally, emotionally and physically exhausted from bitterness and harms that I am holding on to?

Are my days consumed with thoughts of those who have hurt and disrespected me?

What can I do to "discharge" myself from these acts and experiences?

Day 27

There is a difference between powerlessness and being vulnerable. When someone is powerless, there is a sense of feeling incapable and immobilized by their inadequacy, where whatever they are experiencing or witnessing is beyond their control and influence. Being vulnerable, however, is an internal position that requires a choice. This is not about attention seeking or about falling apart. It is when a well-timed release of information can bring about an opportunity for you to grow and bond in your relationships. There is a strong correlation between vulnerability and intimacy. Intimacy is that place in relating where individuals aren't afraid of sharing their deepest selves for fear of rejection. Vulnerability is an invitation to intimacy and is the valve that regulates your emotional exposure. It requires risk and courage but the rewards of stronger, richer, and more intimate relational bonds are worth the risk.

Reflection

Am I guarded in my close relationships? Why?

Am I satisfied with the quality and depth of my relationships?

What can I do to deepen my connection and how I relate to those I love?

Day 28

As human beings, we tend to be thankful only when we experience a reason to be thankful. It is easier to be thankful when you are given a gift or feel considered in some way. The tangible experience is then the determinant for whether or not thankfulness will be expressed. What comes first the chicken or the egg? Does thankfulness allow good things to happen or do good experiences produce thankfulness. I became intrigued with the idea that *cultivating a heart and mindset of thankfulness precedes "good" things happening in life and activates a flow of grace that enhances our ability to outlast challenging times.* Cultivating thankfulness requires an attentiveness to fostering, developing and promoting this mindset. The opposite of cultivating is neglect. Neglecting to be thankful results in self-harm, in that thankless people tend to focus on everything that is not good in their lives. This fixation often leads to poor health, depression, anxiety and countless other life challenges including strained relationships.

Reflection

Why is thankfulness important?

How have I neglected living a thankful life?

What have been the results of my neglect?

Day 29

As you take a panoramic view of your emotions, memories and thoughts, you will find that disappointment, hurt, loss, broken dreams, hurtful and destructive thoughts and memories, insidiously incubate in the deep, and sometimes not so deep, recesses of yourself. They live in boxes tagged "historical evidence" neatly wrapped in many coloured bows of avoidance as you attempt to move forward with your life. As long as your "historical evidence" is allowed to follow you, your desire for change is obstructed. ***What you avoid you incubate but what you challenge and purge leads to change.*** Historical evidence is just that, evidence from your past which is used to justify our current state. Evidence to support your right to be angry, unforgiving or insulated in your misery. Your history only has value when it is working for you. If it is not working for you it is undermining your strength and vision. Any path to freedom starts with a decision, is fueled by courage, supported by corresponding actions, and sustained by intentional living.

Reflection

How important is change to me?

Why must I change?

What am I willing to do to move in the direction of the life I want to have?

Day 30

Resilience is Determined by Asking "How" NOT "Why". The bounce back factor, that ability to recover after life has knocked you on your butt, is controlled by your whys and your how tos. Why did this happen to me? Why did it happen now? Why do bad things happen to good people? These are questions that set us into downward spirals of thought and mood. ***Asking why in situations where you are powerless to change outcomes*** lead to dead end streets. Here anger, chaos, hopelessness, and powerlessness live, rule, and influence your ability to see and choose wisely. If you have experienced a loss of a friendship, job, health, marriage or a loved one, think about how you feel when you constantly ask the question, "why?" Now try asking, "how do I get through the next 15, 30, 45 minutes?" "How do I get through this paperwork?" "How can I get past the divorce?" Observe how you find inner strength by these "how do I?" empowering questions, and how self-pity loses its hold on you. Each day you do this, more ground is covered and your "bounce back" factor will kick in. You will survive, endure, and eventually thrive again. You will be resilient.

Reflection

Am I resilient? If not, why?

What can I do to increase my "bounce back factor"?

Day 31

Existentialism is a philosophical movement that focuses on two major themes, the analysis of human existence and the centrality of human choice. There is a convergence of many beliefs and the emergence of a belief that as human beings we are more than our brains and that we exist for more than just a biological and scientific reason. There is a sense that we are on the planet for something greater than ourselves and that somehow *we have to make meaning of the chaos in a complex world.* Many of us work so hard to survive life till old age that we stop living life. The most impacting people on humanity are those who turned tragedy into triumph and those who came to learn that despite their pain, loss, and oppression, they could make a difference in life and make meaning out of their pain. Nelson Mandela, Martin Luther King, Victor Frankl, Mahatma Gandhi, Joan of Arc, Maya Angelou, Rosa Parks and Amelia Earhart, to name a few, are those who taught us how to use adversity as fuel to climb higher and go farther. These people did not die old, they died empty. They did what they arrived on the planet to do and left a legacy of hope and change that will serve humanity for generations to come. Think about what is that "burr in your saddle." What is that thing that irritates you and frustrates you most? Is it injustice? Is it poverty? Is it a failing school system? Is it broken families? You identify your passion and you will find your purpose. Make a decision to stop surviving your life and start living it today!

Reflection

Are you surviving life instead of living it?

Are you doing what you arrived on the planet to do?

Are you confused about why you are here and what your life is about?

"A choice whether positive or negative sets into motion a course of events that cannot be altered until you make a better choice."

-Abby Napora

Endorsements

Napora's daily dose of Vitamin A is bold, playful, insightful – with powerful daily affirmations that provoke and inspire. Reading her words alone provides a conscientious way of being and shaping one's sense of self into an intentioned and personalized existence. Taking this journey will transform your mental, emotional and physical health and provide a rich vehicle to record and reflect your growth and development. "Embrace the struggle in a way that will allow your body, mind and spirit to enter this new place that is designed to reveal your strength, bring you joy and fulfillment, and allow you to experience new life." Napora's intelligence and compassion for others is simply brilliant.
Valerie Hruschak, MSW, RSW

We all have a best version of ourselves. A version where we are healthy, balanced and connected to our personal goals and the role we can play in our community and society. Unfortunately, life sometimes takes us on a detour away from this path. Abby Napora's Daily dose of vitamin A is a practical guide not only to lead us back to this life path, but gives us the encouragement to stay the course and to make a concerted effort to follow it through to completion and CHANGE. Change that can be permanent and fulfilling. Make the decision and commit to the three month challenge and change the course of your life!
Doctor Marissa Van Der Vyver, MBChB DA (SA) CCFP

Abby has created a simple and intriguing 31 day program to support her readers to live in their full potential. Each day she introduces a concept, grounding it in everyday life and inviting us to stop and consider our own response to it. The questions that follow provide an opportunity for us to explore our own beliefs, experience and desires. Abby's very practical approach challenges us to reflect on our lives and, in doing so, get clearer on how we show up in the world. I believe this innovative program will be a useful tool for anyone wanting to explore and move towards their life's goals.
Morag Reid, Transformational Life Coach

Abby Napora has just delivered an amazing gift to us all including those of us in the martial arts world. Learning to control our thoughts, actions and emotions is fundamental to any martial artist. As we each struggle to rise above life's challenges we need a boost in the right direction and the 31 day journey inside this book is essential for anyone who wants to be truly emotionally and spiritually free. All of my black belt instructors will be using this resource. Take the 31 day Challenge!
Master Dean Siminoff, 5th Dan - TKD Master Instructor
Founder: Martial Arts For Justice

Over the past 15 years, I have been fortunate enough to complete over 20 books on a variety of topics for a number of large publishers. During the process I have had the opportunity to work and collaborate with many professional and passionate writers, each trying to identify and connect with their audiences. This is not easy to do! What Abby has done with this book is just that. She has clearly conveyed her passion, sincerity and desire to help through her writing. As a fellow writer this is inspiring, and as a reader, her content is motivating, engaging and refreshing. It is a heartfelt and helpful book, which I would not hesitate to share with personal and professional friends.
Mike Harwood, Author

Proceeds from the sale of the book will go to Martial Arts for Justice
www.martialartsforjustice.org **and Nelson Cares** http://nelsoncares.ca/

Made in the USA
Charleston, SC
06 December 2015